Thank You, My Love

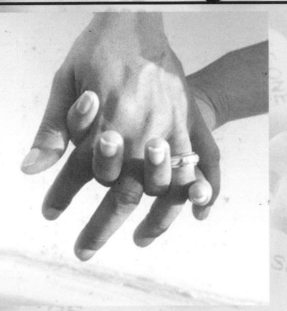

You can personalize this book for your Love!

Find a special photograph!
Lightly glue your photo over the hands and within the border on this page.
Make sure that your photo shows through the window of the book's front cover.

Thank You,
My Love

Everything that I understand,
I understand only because I love.

LEO TOLSTOY

Thank You, My Love

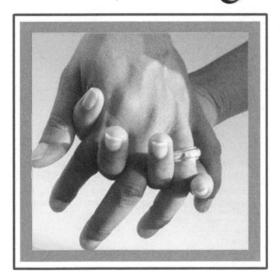

A Keepsake in Celebration of Our Love

SPIRIT PRESS

Thank You, My Love
ISBN 1-40372-034-7

Published in 2005 by Spirit Press, an imprint of Dalmatian Press, LLC.
Copyright © 2005 Dalmatian Press, LLC. Franklin, Tennessee 37067.

Editor: Lila Empson

Writer: Phillip H. Barnhart

Cover and text design: Diane Whisner

05 06 07 LPU 10 9 8 7 6 5 4 3 2 1

*Love is at the center of the
universe, and I am out of
sync when I am not loving.*

MORTON KELSEY

I am giving you a new commandment. Love each other. Just as I have loved you, you should love each other.

JOHN 13:34 NLT

Introduction

My love, since I met you I am much more than I was. You release from me what was there waiting to be spoken to. You deposit in me what I could not have accommodated without your encouragement. You deepen me in the ways of God.

You make me smile when I am tired, and you put life in my steps. You make my world go around, and you make the ride worthwhile. You love me with all your heart and then reach in and get some more. Because of you, I am a journeyer and a discoverer. Because of you, I am a giver and a servant. Because of the way you love me, I begin to understand how much God loves me.

Thank you, my love.

Lead a life of love, just as Christ did.

EPHESIANS 5:2 NIrV

The heart that loves is
always young.

GREEK PROVERB

*Love is our business, and when we don't
love, we are out of business.*

WILLIAM SLOANE COFFIN

*Love can't be forced; it can't be coaxed
or teased. It comes out of heaven,
unmasked and unsought.*

PEARL S. BUCK

*Love is faith internalized
and hope actualized. Love
confirms the authenticity of
our faith and renews the
expectation of our hope.*

ROBERT T. YOUNG

I love all who love me. Those who search for me will surely find me. Unending riches, honor, wealth, and justice are mine to distribute. My gifts are better than the purest gold, my wages better than sterling silver! Those who love me inherit wealth, for I fill their treasuries.

PROVERBS 8:17–21 NLT

*Love that ends is the shadow of
love; true love is without
beginning or end.*

HAZRAT INAYAT KHAN

*There is a land of the living and
a land of the dead and the bridge
is love, the only survival, the
only meaning.*

THORNTON WILDER

One Lover Remembers . . .

I don't remember the first time I saw you in the same way I remember the second time. The first time was at a dinner party where mutual friends introduced us. The second time was in church when those friends invited you to sing in the choir. I remember getting my hymnal out of the rack, looking up, and seeing you in a bright purple robe with the sun shining on you from the back stained-glass window. You looked radiant.

You still do, every time I see you. When we go out on our weekly date. When you hold one of our children in your arms. And when you sing praises to God in the choir.

Thank you, my love.

*Kiss me again and again, for your
love is sweeter than wine.*

Song of Songs 1:2 NLT

Love sought is good, but given unsought is better.

William Shakespeare

*Spread love everywhere you go.
First of all in your own house,
give love to your children, to
your wife or husband, to a
next-door neighbor. Let no one
ever come to you without leaving
better and happier.*

MOTHER TERESA

*It isn't the great big pleasures that count the most;
it's making a great deal out of the little ones.*

JEAN WEBSTER

It is only with the heart that one can see rightly.

ANTOINE DE SAINT-EXUPÉRY

Do not abandon wisdom,
and she will protect you;
love her, and she will
keep you safe.

PROVERBS 4:6 GNT

Your only treasures are
those which you carry in
your heart.

DEMOPHILUS

Love one another as he commanded us.

1 JOHN 3:23 NIV

You have shown great and steadfast love to your servant my father David, because he walked before you in faithfulness.

1 KINGS 3:6 NRSV

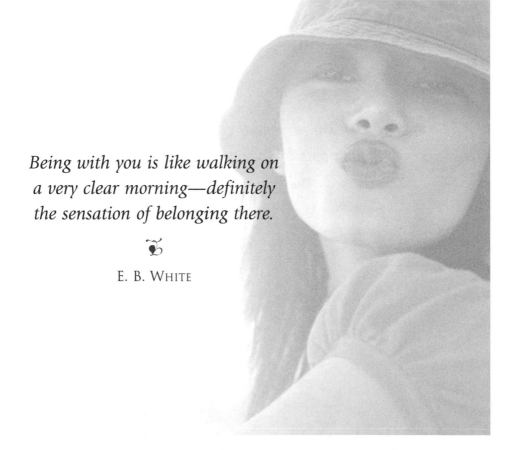

*Being with you is like walking on
a very clear morning—definitely
the sensation of belonging there.*

E. B. WHITE

21

If you surrender completely to the moments as they pass, you live more richly those moments.

ANNE MORROW LINDBERGH

Did You Know?

Kids Say Love Is . . .

When someone loves you, the way they say your name is different. Billy, age 4

Love is when a girl puts on perfume and a boy puts on shaving cologne and they go out and smell each other. Karl, age 5

Love is when you go out to eat and give somebody most of your French fries without making them give you any of theirs. Chrissy, age 6

Love is when Mommy gives Daddy the best piece of chicken. Elaine, age 5

Live a life of love, just as
Christ loved us and gave
himself up for us.

EPHESIANS 5:2 NIV

Line by line, moment by moment, special times are etched into our memories in the permanent ink of everlasting love in our relationships.

GLORIA GAITHER

All that is worth cherishing
begins in the heart.

SUZANNE CHAPIN

Recall it as often as you wish, a
happy memory never wears out.

LIBBIE FUDIM

*Love is a medicine for the sickness
of the world; a prescription often
given, too rarely taken.*

KARL A. MENNINGER

As far as I can see, love is a combination of admiration, respect, and passion. If you have one of those going, that's about par for the course. If you have two, you aren't quite world class, but you're close. If you have all three, then you don't need to die; you're already in heaven.

WILLIAM WHARTON

Love consists in this, that two solitudes protect and touch and greet each other.

RAINER MARIA RILKE

Our Lord gave us his love not in order that we might be loved, but that we might love one another.

REUEL L. HOWE

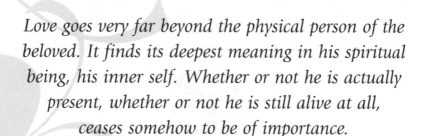

Love goes very far beyond the physical person of the beloved. It finds its deepest meaning in his spiritual being, his inner self. Whether or not he is actually present, whether or not he is still alive at all, ceases somehow to be of importance.

VICTOR FRANKL

Survival Tip

*S*teps of an Encouragement Meeting:

- Meet in a place where you won't be interrupted.
- Sit facing each other, close enough to hold hands.
- One partner begins by saying, "Something I appreciated about you today was . . ."
- The listening partner maintains eye contact, never interrupts, then feeds back the feelings expressed without challenging them.
- Switch roles and repeat the process.

*I remember how faithful you
were when you were young,
how you loved me when we
were first married; you
followed me through the
desert, through a land that
had not been planted.*

JEREMIAH 2:2 GNT

*Love is a spendthrift, leaves
its arithmetic at home, is
always "in the red."*

PAUL SCHERER

*If love is blind, love
cannot hit the mark.*

WILLIAM SHAKESPEARE

*I wish you sunshine on your path
and storms to season your journey.*

ROBERT A. WARD

*The best way to light up
the world is with a
current of love.*

Sandy Bennett

Since love is not a thing, it is not lost when given. You can offer your love completely to hundreds of people and still retain the same love you had originally. It is like knowledge. The wise man can teach all he knows and when he's through he'll still know all that he has taught.

LEO BUSCAGLIA

Love Climbs High

A legend tells about an eagle swooping down and carrying a little baby to its lofty perch. The strong men of the village tried to scale the high and rugged cliff, but each in his own turn failed. Then past them came a slight and frail woman. She climbed the sheer precipice systematically and, after a long time, returned, bringing the baby down in a shawl. How did she do it? everyone asked in amazement. How did she scale such a height and return safely with the child? She told them the secret: "I am the baby's mother." Her love outdistanced the strength of all the others.

Love enables you to do great things.

*See how great a love the Father
has bestowed on us, that we
should be called the
children of God.*

1 JOHN 3:1 NASB

*Love is the aim of my life,
the reason for my existence,
the only thing that really
satisfies me.*

Carlo Carretto

Perfect love means to love the one through whom one became unhappy.

Sören Kierkegaard

The trick is to love somebody. If you love one person, you see everybody else differently.

James Baldwin

*Anywhere you go, let me
go too. Love me, that's
all I ask of you.*

ANDREW LLOYD WEBBER

*You have heard that it was said,
"Love your friends, hate your
enemies." But now I tell you: love
your enemies and pray for those
who persecute you, so that you
may become the children of
your Father in heaven.*

MATTHEW 5:43–45 GNT

There aren't enough people in the world who can say they love you often enough to make you start loving yourself, if you don't love yourself to begin with.

G. RICHARD HOARD

Unable are the loved to die, for love is immortality.

EMILY DICKINSON

One Lover Remembers...

I remember the week we were married and I was making room for some books on a shelf. On the shelf was a vase you'd had since you were a little girl. I dropped the vase, and the unforgiving tile floor broke it into many pieces. I gasped, moaned, and then cried out. You came running into the den, expecting to see me crumpled down with a premature heart attack, but I stood quite erect looking at the smashed vase through wet eyes. You laughed. That took me aback, and I protested your mood. You laughed again and said, "Honey, it's just a thing." Then I laughed, and from that day, I have known what is important in life.

Thank you, my love.

Jesus looked at him and loved him.
MARK 10:21 NIV

*Love is the will to extend one's self
for the purpose of nurturing one's
own or another's spiritual growth.*

M. SCOTT PECK

Some say love, it is a river
that drowns the tender reed.
Some say love, it is a razor that leaves
your heart to bleed.
Some say love, it is a hunger,
an endless aching need.
I say love, it is a flower
and you its only seed.

Amanda McBroom

The difference between a lady and a flower girl is not how she behaves but how she is treated.

Eliza Doolittle

We do not find love by looking for it. We find love by giving it.

Reuel L. Howe

Don't just pretend that you love others. Really love them.

ROMANS 12:9 NLT

*Many a heart is hungry
for a little word of love.*

Ebenezer E. Rexford

*Honor your father and mother. Love
your neighbor as yourself.*

MATTHEW 19:19 NLT

*Plant the good seeds of
righteousness, and you will
harvest a crop of my love.*

HOSEA 10:12 NLT

Life is a journey from the cradle to the grave. Only one thing is required: that, along the way, we love.

IRVING STONE

Hope won't wait without love. Those two are twins.

DAVID A. REDDING

Did You Know?

*K*ids Also Say Love Is . . .

When my grandmother got arthritis, she couldn't bend over and paint her toenails anymore. So my grandfather does it for her. That's love. Rebecca, age 8

Love is when my mommy makes coffee for my daddy and she takes a sip before giving it to him, to make sure it tastes okay. Danny, age 7

Love is what's in the room with you at Christmas if you stop opening presents and listen. Bobby, age 7

You have been called to live in freedom—not freedom to satisfy your sinful nature, but freedom to serve one another in love.

GALATIANS 5:13 NLT

When she holds me, she enfolds me in her world.

HARRY CHAPIN

Love is not so much a gazing at each other as a looking outward together, in the same direction.

THOMAS A. HARRIS

Love each other or perish.

W. H. AUDEN

*Love is discovery without end. When
the searching dies, the love dies.*

EARNEST LARSEN

I love you for the part of me you bring out. I love you for putting your hand into my heaped-up heart and passing over all the foolish, weak things that you can't help dimly seeing there and for drawing out into the light all the beautiful belongings no one else had looked quite far enough to find.

AUTHOR UNKNOWN

"Jonathan," he said, and these were the last
words he spoke, "keep working on love."
RICHARD BACH

*True love never runs smooth unless the
lovers are good shock absorbers.*

FAITH TYNDALE

Love has the hands to help others. It has the feet to hasten to the poor and the needy. It has the eyes to see misery and want. It has the ears to hear the sighs and sorrows of others. That is what love looks like.

SAINT AUGUSTINE OF HIPPO

Survival Tip

*W*ays to Improve a Relationship:

- Develop the courage to be imperfect.

- Schedule times to be alone together.

- Set aside regular times for fun each week.

- Don't be judgmental.

- Develop shared dreams, goals, and interests.

- Adopt realistic expectations.

- Make decisions jointly.

*As I passed by again, I saw
that the time had come for
you to fall in love.*

EZEKIEL 16:8 GNT

The gift of love is forever
absolute. It will never be obsolete.

HELEN PETTIT

Love is a decision, not an emotion.

JIM WRIGHT

*I prefer to think of love as something
we grow into, not something we
fall in and out of.*

LEO BUSCAGLIA

We love you, God, and that's the wisest thing we've ever done.

JEANETTE CLIFT-GEORGE

Some day, after humankind has harnessed every other form of energy, we will finally learn how to harness the power of love. When we turn to doing that, for the second time in the history of the world we will have discovered fire.

PIERRE TEILHARD DE CHARDIN

Love Accepts All

A young man and woman were in love just before the Civil War broke out and were to be married. When war came, however, he had to go to battle. One day a letter came from the soldier. It said someone else was writing for him because he had lost both arms. In the letter, he released her from their commitment to marry. She got on the first train and went to find him. When she saw him in the hospital, she threw her arms around his neck and said, "These arms and hands will take care of you. I will never let you go. I love you so much." True love accepts limitations.

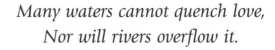

Many waters cannot quench love,
Nor will rivers overflow it.

SONG OF SOLOMON 8:7 NASB

*We may affirm absolutely that
nothing great in the world has
been accomplished without passion.*

Friedrich Hegel

69

Blessed are the ones God sends
to show his love for us.

LINDA KARSTEN

The loveliest faces are to be seen by
moonlight, when one sees half with
the eye and half with the fancy.

PERSIAN PROVERB

*True love comes quietly, without
banners or flashing lights. If you
hear bells, get your ears checked.*

ERICH SEGAL

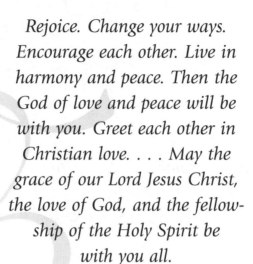

*Rejoice. Change your ways.
Encourage each other. Live in
harmony and peace. Then the
God of love and peace will be
with you. Greet each other in
Christian love. . . . May the
grace of our Lord Jesus Christ,
the love of God, and the fellow-
ship of the Holy Spirit be
with you all.*

2 Corinthians 13:11–13 NLT

Romance is too egocentric to be love.

TONY COMPOLO

*I show affection for you every time
I pay attention to you.*

JIM KERN

One Lover
Remembers . . .

I remember that we spent money that we didn't have on our twenty-fifth anniversary. We chose an exotic place that has forever been in the romantic hall of fame. White sand, blue water, and sunsets that took our breath away. A five-star hotel and the best of restaurants. Horse-drawn carriages pulling us slowly down picture-card streets and waterfalls under which we played like children. That night at the outdoor opera, no matter how old I get, will never fade from my memory. I'll never forget the flight home high above the clouds.

Let's do it again, okay?

*Mercy, peace, and love be
yours in abundance.*

JUDE 1:2 NIV

*A successful marriage is an edifice
that must be rebuilt every day.*

ANDRÉ MAUROIS

What greater thing is there for two human souls, than to feel that they are joined for life— to strengthen each other in all labor, to rest on each other for all sorrow, to minister to each other in all pain, to be one with each other in silent unspeakable memories at the moment of the last parting?

GEORGE ELIOT

Love reduces friction to a fraction.

PHYLLIS ALDERSON

*A marriage kept on the back burner
will die from lack of heat.*

HEATHER MORRIS

Your love for one another will prove to the world that you are my disciples.

John 13:35 NLT

A successful marriage isn't finding the right person; it's being the right person.

WAYMAN TOLBERT

*Jacob was in love with Rachel, so he said
[to her father], "I will work seven years for you,
if you will let me marry Rachel."*

GENESIS 29:18 GNT

*As a bridegroom rejoices over his bride,
so will your God rejoice over you.*

ISAIAH 62:5 NIV

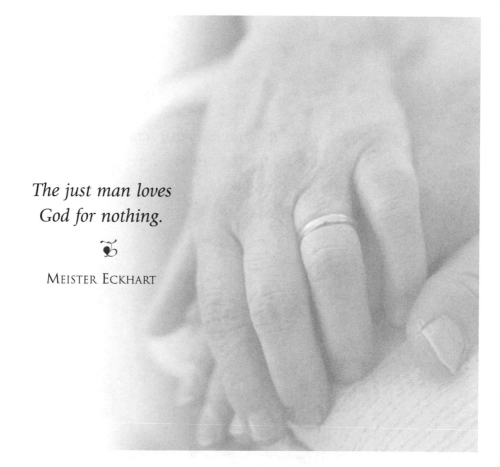

*The just man loves
God for nothing.*

MEISTER ECKHART

*Happy marriages begin when
we marry the one we love
and blossom when we love
the one we marry.*

AUTHOR UNKNOWN

Did You Know?

*K*ids Say This About Marriage . . .

You got to find somebody who likes the same stuff. Like, if you like sports, she should like it if you like sports, and she should keep the chips and dip coming. Alan, age 10

No person really decides before they grow up who they're going to marry. God decides it all the way before, and you get to find out later who you're stuck with. Kirsten, age 10

No age is good to get married at. You got to be a fool to get married. Freddie, age 6

How beautiful you are, my love;
how your eyes shine with love!

Song of Songs 1:15 gnt

A good wife laughs at her husband's jokes not because they are clever, but because she is.

PORTER ADAMS

By all means marry; if you get a good wife, you will become happy; if you get a bad one, you will become a philosopher.

SOCRATES

A successful marriage is when a couple lives happily even after.

JENNY PASS

*Nothing in this world bears
the impress of the Son of
God so surely as forgiveness.*

ALICE CARY

I didn't marry you because you were perfect. I didn't even marry you because I loved you. I married you because you gave me a promise. The promise made up for your faults. And the promise I gave you made up for mine. Two imperfect people got married, and it was the promise that made the marriage.

THORNTON WILDER

We cannot cure the world of sorrows,
but we can choose to live in joy.

JOSEPH CAMPBELL

Find joy in everything that leads to God.

SAINT THERESA OF AVILA

Rachel and I are not given to sloppy sentimentalism. But we can honestly say that each of us has stood at the center of the other's existence; that we have honored and loved each other; that we have never broken our marriage contract; and that we wouldn't trade a day of it—not the sorrow or joys—for all the gold in the world.

JACKIE ROBINSON

Survival Tip

*H*ow to Handle Relationship Conflicts:

- Show mutual respect. Attitude is more important than anything else.

- Pinpoint the real issue. You may be arguing about the kids or money, but the real issue may be about who is in control.

- Seek areas of agreement. Consider aspects where you already think alike.

- Focus on the present and the future. Don't derail the process by going back to the past.

All this is from God, who reconciled us to himself through Christ, and has given us the ministry of reconciliation.

2 CORINTHIANS 5:18 NRSV

*Bad times have a
value. These are
occasions a good
learner will not miss.*

RALPH WALDO EMERSON

He who won't be counseled can't be helped.

BENJAMIN FRANKLIN

*Good advice is no better than bad advice
unless it is taken at the right time.*

DANISH PROVERB

If God had a wallet, your photo would be in it.

AUTHOR UNKNOWN

What makes a happy marriage? It is a question which all men and women ask one another. The answer is to be found, I think, in the mutual discovery, by two who marry, of the deepest need of the other's personality, and the satisfaction of that need.

PEARL S. BUCK

Liking and Loving

*I*n the movie *Shenandoah*, young Sam asks Mr. Anderson for permission to marry his daughter. Mr. Anderson asks Sam why he wants to do that, and Sam replies, "Well . . . uh . . . I love her." Mr. Anderson says, "That's not good enough, Sam." Then he explains. "When I married Jenny's mother, I didn't love her; I liked her. I liked her a whole lot. I liked Martha for three years after we married, and then it dawned on me that I loved her. I still do. Sam, when you love a woman without liking her, the nights can be long and cold, and contempt comes up with the sun."

It's easier to grow to love someone you like than to keep loving someone you don't like.

He took Rebekah, and she became his wife; and he loved her.

GENESIS 24:67 NRSV

*God loves each of us, as if
there is only one of us.*

SAINT AUGUSTINE OF HIPPO

*The biggest heresy in marriage
is alphabetical: Big I, little u.
Marriage needs a Big We.*

MAXIE DUNNAM

*Love is true when you don't see
eye to eye but can still walk
hand in hand.*

FRAN HAMPTON

*A successful marriage
requires falling in love
many times with the
same person.*

HOYT STADMAN

Love one another with mutual affection; outdo one another in showing honor. Do not lag in zeal, be ardent in spirit, serve the Lord. Rejoice in hope, be patient in suffering, persevere in prayer. Contribute to the needs of the saints; extend hospitality to strangers.

ROMANS 12:10–13 NRSV

Love is a decision, not an emotion.

DENNIS FRANKUM

Marriage is a both a sacrament of God's love for his people and an extension of that love.

G. K. CHESTERTON

One Lover
Remembers...

I remember wondering if you could get along with my mother. She wasn't easy to get along with. I grew up with her and knew her ways, but I wondered how you, coming from the family you did, would be able to take her. Before I took you home to meet my family for the first time, I decided to talk to you about my mother. I wanted to know if you could love her, and you assured me you could, and you have all these years. I remember when I wondered out loud later how you could have done that and you replied, "Well, she's your mother, isn't she?"

Thank you, my love.

*You shall be together even
in the silent memory of God.*
KAHLIL GIBRAN

*Every soul that loves lives in the heart
of God and hears him speak.*

AUTHOR UNKNOWN

The goal of oneness can be almost frightening when we realize that God does not intend only that my wife and I find our personal needs met in marriage. He also wants our relationship to validate the claims of Christianity to a watching world as an example of the power of Christ's redeeming love to overcome the divisive effects of sin.

LARRY CRABB

A marriage needs love. And God.
And a little money. That's all.
The rest you can deal with.

JAMES MCBRIDE

The goal in marriage is not to think
alike but to think together.

AUTHOR UNKNOWN

Grow old along with me!
The best is yet to be.

ROBERT BROWNING

*Courage is the ability
to choose the best out
of the worst.*

MAX CLELAND

Be strong and take heart,
*all you who hope in the L*ORD.

PSALM 31:24 NIV

The joy of the Lord is my strength.

NEHEMIAH 8:10 NRSV

*Time given to inner
renewal is never wasted*

HENRI J. M. NOUWEN

She had been like a caterpillar in a cocoon, and he had drawn her out and shown her she was a butterfly.

KEN FOLLETT

Did You Know?

*K*ids Also Say This About Marriage…

Twenty-three is the best age to get married, because by then you know the person forever. Camille, age 10

If you kiss someone, you should marry them and have kids with them. Howard, age 8

To make marriage work, tell your wife she looks pretty even if she looks like a truck. Ricky, age 10

You can tell if two people are married if they are yelling at the same kids. Derrick, age 8

*I hear about your love
for all of God's people.*

PHILEMON 1:5 NIrV

Receive what cheer you may. The night is long that never finds the day.

WILLIAM SHAKESPEARE

Hope is the parent of faith.

C. A. BARTOL

*A necessity is a luxury that
has gained a foothold.*

DOUG LARSON

A person's real needs are very simple. You must learn to live with yourself, with others, and with God.

DAVID WILKERSON

117

He drew a circle and shut me out.
Heretic, rebel, a thing to flout.
But love and I had the wit to win.
We drew a circle and brought him in.

EDWIN MARKHAM

Don't ever be married.
Always be marrying.
MOLLY O'CONNELL

The math of marriage is one
plus one equals one.
JAMES THURMAN

The very least you can do in your life is figure out what you hope for. And the most you can do is live inside that hope. Not admire it from a distance, but live right in it, under its roof.

BARBARA KINGSOLVER

Survival Tip

*C*ommunication Checkup:

- Do I willingly set aside time to talk?

- When I disagree, do I stay on the issue?

- Do I see my mate's point of view?

- Am I dogmatic, condescending, argumentative, or egocentric?

- Do I monopolize our conversations?

- Do I try to make my mate feel guilty?

- Do I withdraw in the midst of conflict?

- Am I an interested listener?

- Do I overuse the words *always, never,* and *every time?*

- Am I kind?

*Your love delights me,
my sweetheart and bride.
Your love is better than
wine; your perfume more
fragrant than any spice.*

SONG OF SONGS 4:10 GNT

*The moments when you
have really lived are the
moments when you did
things in the spirit of love.*

HENRY DRUMMOND

Trust is the start of it, joy is part of it,
love is at the heart of it.

AUTHOR UNKNOWN

Life is like a prism; what you see
depends on how you turn the glass.

JONATHAN KELLERMAN

*Love is patient; love is kind;
love is not envious or
boastful or arrogant or
rude. It does not insist on
its own way; it is not
irritable or resentful;
it does not rejoice in
wrongdoing, but rejoices
in the truth. It bears all
things, believes all things,
hopes all things, endures all
things. Love never ends.*

1 Corinthians 13:4–8 NRSV

Aladdin Books
Macmillan Publishing Company
866 Third Avenue, New York, NY 10022

Published simultaneously by Methuen
Children's Books, Ltd., London

Printed in Hong Kong
by Wing King Tong Co Ltd

10   9   8   7   6   5   4   3   2   1

ISBN 0-689-71195-6

Cataloging-in-Publication Data is available.

A FABLE BY AESOP

Wolf! Wolf!

Retold and illustrated by Gerald Rose

Aladdin Books
Macmillan Publishing Company
New York

The boy who looked after the goats
enjoyed playing practical jokes.
When he was bored and lonely...

he would shout, "Wolf! Wolf!"

and all the villagers would run up the hill with sticks and weapons.

He did this many times, so that his friends and neighbors grew tired of his games and were not pleased to be given such a fright.

One day a real wolf appeared among the goats.

The boy shouted, "Wolf! Wolf! Help! The wolf is attacking the goats."

and the wolf made off with his supper.

People who do not always tell the truth
will not always be believed.